With questions come answers so choose wisely.

Affluent MINDS

CORE EXPRESSIONS *for a* RICH *and* WONDERFUL LIFE

A N N E   A R V I Z U

ARCHWAY PUBLISHING

Archway Publishing books may be ordered
through booksellers or by contacting:

Archway Publishing
1663 Liberty Drive
Bloomington, IN 47403
www.archwaypublishing.com
1 (888) 242-5904

ISBN: 978-1-4808-9129-6 (sc)
ISBN: 978-1-4808-9130-2 (e)

Library of Congress Control Number: 2020908830

Print information available on the last page.

Archway Publishing rev. date: 07/10/2020

DEDICATION

To the Heroes of 2020, our frontline leaders who never had a pause during this epic pause. My gratitude to all healthcare professionals, supermarket workers, delivery personnel, and so many other essential workers who daily choose the dance of affluence, which is ultimately to spur one another on to love and good deeds.

Thank you.

And to my family and friends—all of you, past and present—who have encouraged my writing, and especially to you, Jaime, my husband and all-time rock, for the space and support in this quarantine time to write. As Gibran writes in *The Prophet*, "For the pillars of the temple stand apart. And the oak tree and the cypress grow not in each other's shadow."

Thank you.

Affluence is our birthright.
—Anne Arvizu

CONTENTS

INTRODUCTION

Life bombards us. It was already too much, too fast all the time, even before 2020's new normal of global hyperconnectivity. And I have some real news for you: Even though life may return to a semblance of normal, it's in make-or-break times like this when leadership is defined.

Every day, the thoughts we think, the words we speak, the company we keep, the decisions we make, and the actions we take will guide us toward or away from success, love, power, and peace. In response to the COVID-19 global pandemic, my hope in writing this book is to inspire and encourage you to tap into your inherent core-centered nature, which is the very spirit that will help you rise, recover, and stay strong no matter the circumstance. In the midst of darkness, light shines, leadership rises, and those worthy to be used for good will surface as change agents. As they say, the cream always rises to the top. And love always wins.

What do people say of great leaders? How do they describe them? Mother Teresa was selfless. Mahatma Gandhi was steadfast. Jesus was controversial. Reflecting on who we are inside determines our self-worth and our willingness to truly lead.

It is my hope that by reading this book, something is sparked inside of you. Perhaps it's a return to core values, and even a return to Love itself. Perhaps it's a pivot you have been meaning to make in your business, a transition you are in, a habit you need to give up, or an attitude that needs adjustment.

Incorporate these disciplines into your life, so you can:

- get balanced
- live in high productivity mode
- get laser beam-focused
- break through negative mindsets
- quit believing the lie that opposes your biggest dream
- become more self-aware of empowering choices and actions
- shift every negative thought to a positive force for good
- enter your core, so co-creative ideas and energy flow
- manage time like a CEO
- and more…

It's my vision to see leaders like you, in executive positions, or at the helm of public facing businesses, shatter every ceiling by being raised to a higher standard of living and personal core power expression in alignment with your values and purpose. I will present the mindset of affluence, as well as highlight success disciplines leveraged with the power of coaching to define them in a fresh way. By shedding some light on what makes a good leader, it is my hope that you will also unravel the many layers and beliefs that you have assimilated through your life's journey. Rekindle core values that make you and the world better and shed conflicting and disempowering ones once and for all. I believe this will support you in bringing self-awareness to some simple mental choices you can make as a leader to become a more effective influencer and communicator. Finally, I hope to strike a chord resonant with your heart of hearts. Because it's there in the very seat of your essence where your power for positive change lies and where life-balance is possible.

PART 1

Transforming Your Mindset

CHAPTER 1

Thoughts, Words, & Deeds

THE THOUGHTS WE THINK

It begins with a seed. In a vulnerable, quiet moment, a negative question seeps through. Then another. And another. The barrage of negative questions can sound like this on a deep and almost imperceptible level: *What if it doesn't happen? What if I go broke and can never retire? What if I catch the deadly virus? Is this the end of the world?*

Our inner dialogue races to answer the incoming questions that come from the fear mechanism in our amygdala. It was there in our reptilian brain, under our neocortex and cortex, that our ancestors received physiological cues for flight or fight, and we still use that part of our brain today as a means of keeping ourselves safe. But we can choose to answer from that place or choose a better question to put the negative one in its place.

These fear thoughts swirl in the waters of our mind, and if not held captive, will eventually expand and pressurize inside our heads until they escape through our mouths.

THE WORDS WE SPEAK

Our words are powerful and shape our world. Once you get in conversation about the negative, it begins to have a life of its own—a ripple effect like an echo that scatters with new questions and statements. *What do you think we should do? This is bad, really bad, right? Do we go to the supermarket and clear out the toilet paper?* The choice hangs in the balance to act or negate the questions aloud.

THE COMPANY WE KEEP

We all have them—the naysayers, the pull-you-downers, the energetic manipulators at work or at home. Are you listening to them or listening to your inner guidance? Are you listening to the naysayers and pull-you-downers around you or to those who pull you up and say you can?

Being affected by others is one of the primary reasons that in times of stress, such as being homebound with family members, kids, pets, and the people around us may have become a source of friction, resulting in stressful situations. Is it their fault? No. We have the choice to pull from the font of core values and emotions that give us power. We have the choice to become the thermostat, and not the thermometer, so that we set the temperature of our atmosphere.

THE THINGS WE DO

We start writing out our will, crying as we do, and telling others about our wishes for our funerals and who gets what. We run to the supermarket and fill our carts with all the things.

I know. I get it. We *all* go there. But the good news

is that we all can instantly flip the script and choose new questions, words, company, and actions.

With questions come answers, so choose wisely.

Affluence is an all-encompassing mindset that begins with thoughts and deep inner beliefs and knowing. You are completely connected to your creator, and you are richer in thought, word, and deed than you can imagine. That thing or goal or state of being you desire? It's already yours.

It simply requires activating leadership principles, emotional states, and core values that you can choose and use any day. You have to think a certain way to be a certain way.

CHAPTER 2
Defining Your Affluent Mind

On a daily basis, you can choose the qualities of affluence. In doing so, you shape your life for contribution and meaning, and you ensure success in that service. Ultimately, these qualities are adjectives that describe a servant leader. The most iconic and best-loved leaders of all time share these attributes. Although it's not an exhaustive list, it's a great starting point for creating a full and prosperous life. Use this list as a mirror and choose to water the seeds of each quality in your own life so they continue to grow. You will see that those nasty old negative questions begin to lose their power as the responses become governed by the unlimited potential of your affluent mind. When you lead from your C-O-R-E—which stands for Centered, Open, Resilient, and Energized—everything is possible. The word *core* is the basis of an acronym I believe in so much that I trademarked it. These positive C-O-R-E-4 are the polar opposites of the negative C-O-R-E-4 (chaos, overwhelm, resistance and exhaustion) that surround us in every news report. We can either let the darkness creep in and douse our light, or we can choose to be lit from within.

The difference is the mindset we carry daily. Are we of service? Do we give out of overflow? Are we change agents? When you carry out a purpose-driven life, you know you're meant to be an agent of change. The attributes that follow are the result of your core-centered life.

Affluent
Faithful
Free
Loving
Understanding
Expectant
Nourishing
Thoughtful

Motivated
Inquiring
Notable
Dedicated
Serving

Now, let's assimilate a new understanding of each word in light of living a joy-filled, prosperous life.

A

Is for Affluent

In our modern times, if we were sitting at a café having a conversation, and we used the descriptor of *affluent* to describe a mutual friend, any nearby listener would immediately assume we were speaking about someone rich. The person in question may possibly be, but the archaic definition and root of this state of mind referred to the free and abundant flow of water. Picture a stream of clear, life-giving water rushing down a mountain as ice melts in the spring. When you have an affluent mind, you act as a river, not a reservoir, allowing your highest good to flow outward in service to others.

Affluence, therefore, is our inherent core state of receiving and giving.

F

Is for Faithful

Faithful quite literally means "full of faith." Faith is related to having a sense of security with regard to the object of your faith. If the object of your faith is God, it means you believe he will take care of you. If the object of your faith is the lamp on your desk, you believe the electricity will flow when you turn on that lamp as long as it's in working order. When you show up as a faithful spouse, you use this quality in reverse, promising to always be there for the other person.

Faith is our inherent core state of safety and protection.

F

Is for Free

Those who are free in their minds are unencumbered by the thoughts or comments of others and are able to take action easily and despite opposition. If Joan has an exciting idea for a new business venture and she begins to tell people about it, some may encourage her to do it while others may be neutral. But chances are, if the majority of people around Joan are not entrepreneurs, they won't understand why she'd want to use her time, money, and effort to create a product or service that they personally feel isn't needed.

To be free means to be self-governed or autonomous. We value freedom from slavery, yet some tormented souls succumb to the six-inch, internal, self-inflicted prison between both ears.

Freedom is our core state of being unlimited.

L

Is for Loving

When Sara Blakely founded Spanx, she made her first product out of a need she had. She simply wanted to wear white pants without any lines showing underneath, and then she decided to create more for others. At first, she went door to door. Later, she went nation to nation. Loving others is an expression of outpouring. If *love* is another word for God, then being loving is a natural expression of care and compassion for yourself and others. Love will enable a woman to lift a car to save her at-risk child.

Love magnified is your ultimate core power.

U

Is for Understanding

When you are tolerant, sympathetic, or empathetic to the plight of another human, you exhibit the quality of understanding. It means there is a knowing, intelligent force within that can filter what they see, good and bad, pros and cons, and come to a higher level of harmony or relationship. I always tell people to take in the meat and spit out the bones. There is a liberty that does not require censorship because when knowledge and wisdom come together, understanding can be formed.

Understanding is our core force for meaning, value, and significance.

E

Is for Expectant

An expectant mother awaits her child. An expectant author awaits the day he or she sees his or her book in print and the day of its first sale. Neither of these parties gets anything out of it. On the contrary, they put a lot of work in. That's why they call it labor. They wait in joyful hope to see the baby's face, to hear the laughter of the boy or girl they carried, to see the cover of the book, or to get their first review, knowing their words meant something and changed a reader's life for the better. Ultimately, hope says what I produce matters, and what I want to achieve will come to pass.

Expectation anchors core values to our souls.

N

Is for Nourishing

At the most basic level, our current paradigm tells us that nourishment has a lot to do with food and the nutritious components of that food. We can either eat empty calories in a bag of cheese puffs or sit down among friends and family before a healthful, warm, clean meal. The choice is ours to be nourished or not. The choice is also ours to be a nourishing force to all we encounter. Great leaders develop others, and as a result, nurture comes into their lives.

Nourishment is a core requirement for growth.

T

Is for Thoughtful

We think of someone as thoughtful when they pick out great gifts that the recipient would love. Instead of rushing around a crowded mall filled with bah–humbug attitudes and picking out what's on sale out of what's left, cheerful givers do the opposite. They heed the needs and wants of others, think their gifts through, and order them in advance.

Thoughtfulness is an expression of kindness at your core.

Is for Motivated

Here's a little history lesson. The first known use of the word *motivated* was in 1903. It's a modern term used in this past century. We all know that we can have good or bad motives, but to be motivated means to have a strong desire to do well or attain success in any given endeavor. Its very nature and definition are positive. Choosing excellence is a matter of the will tied to a greater cause.

Motivation is our core stimulus for success.

I

Is for Inquiring

The early bird pecks about and finds its worm. Sherlock Holmes always gets his villain. All those who seek answers will be rewarded. Today, the art and science of using questions is called *coaching*. A mentor might tell you exactly what to do, and a consultant can create the process around how to get there. But a good coach does not impose his or her values or viewpoint. In professional coaching, one of the presuppositions is that the client has the answers within. That means if I'm coaching you and I know you have the best answers inside you, it's my job to be wildly curious and nonjudgmental as I relentlessly ask the right questions to root those answers out. Sometimes, it takes just one question to unlock a mental padlock or to dissipate a longstanding fear.

Inquisitiveness at your core brings freedom from judgment.

N

Is for Notable

In medicine, we use the word *remarkable* to notate a lab value that is out of range. When a lab value is not within normal limits, it generally means that something is wrong. As in so many cases, the way we use our words is often different from their actual definitions. A notable author is distinguished and prominent in his or her circle of influence. If you were ever in a physics class and you watched the video of the Tacoma Narrows Bridge, later nicknamed "Galloping Gertie," and its spectacular, oscillating collapse, you may recall that there was a time when bridges weren't stable enough to endure high winds or vibrations. A notable engineering achievement, therefore, was the design of the new bridge that included dramatic capacity improvements. A notable life, in the true sense, means you've made an impact and left a legacy to be proud of.

Notability is at the core of innovation.

D

Is for Dedicated

A dedicated entrepreneur will be persistent until his or her goal is achieved. The reason for that dedication runs deep. To fully devote yourself to a cause requires knowledge of its purpose, the ideals it upholds, and the positive changes it will make. Steve Jobs was a brilliant entrepreneur. He wanted to create computers that were more helpful and equally as beautiful. At one point during his success, he was fired from his own board. He could have walked away and done something else, but when the opportunity arose, with dedication to the vision and a newfound humility during a forced pause, he went back and turned the company and his personal failure around to become a global icon for success.

Dedication is the core decision behind persistence and perseverance.

S

Is for Steady

It is a rare quality in an erratic world to be unfaltering, uniform, genuine, and integral. When we look up at our flag, we have a feeling of pride, principle, and attachment to the values we proclaim to uphold. We all know people who are one way to our face at work but completely different behind our backs with their friends. People can tell when others lie, and they can tell when they're being talked about. True leaders are the same in all situations.

Steadiness in your core is the rudder that steers the ship through all kinds of waves.

CHAPTER 3

The Granite Ceiling is Broken

Congratulations! The glass ceiling is now broken. In fact, it was never there. Since the 1970s, the glass ceiling has been a metaphor with regard to women earning less. But in so many ways, all of us have our own glass ceiling. In some cases, it's made of granite, and it has kept us small and undervalued, as well as safe and protected. Whether it's self-imposed or externally imposed or both, it's up to us to decide to change the paradigm.

No one has forced you to take a pay cut. You have an awareness and understanding of reality in your core. And God has unlimited resources for you in this beautiful earth. So, what is the answer? How do we break free and choose a better response?

Jennifer, a small business owner and client of mine, came to one of our strategy sessions in a bind. She wanted clarity coaching to make a major decision. Her business was going through a downturn, and she was spending multiple sleepless nights mulling over the negative circumstances, trying to figure out her next steps. She admitted to being torn between two potential solutions. One was to move her business into another direction, and the other was to take a job opportunity that just happened to come up. She began to explore both scenarios, and as we spoke, she realized taking the job was an easy way out of her business crisis. It would be an immediate fix for her fear over her financial situation.

As she went through the interview process, it became clear that she would be paid less than even the standards in the marketplace as posted on HR websites. She ended up taking the job at the bottom of the range that was presented to her. She went for the quick fix solution and security. Later, Jennifer found out she was making a quarter less than her male colleagues, even though she tried to negotiate a higher compensation package. Rather than feel like a victim, she made the decision to be content in the security she chose during this 'layover' situation. She would course correct for the future with a narrative that served her based on a core belief that all things, even this temporary injustice, would work for her good in the end. In the journey of life, sometimes there are direct routes to success, and sometimes there are long and uncomfortable layovers.

Then, we all know leaders everyone wants to be around. They magnetize others to them with their positive outlook, daring plans, and easygoing attitude. Kenny was that type. Not a lot ruffled his feathers. I remember a fellow non-profit volunteer smiling as she described him as open-minded and patient. These were obvious traits that were ingrained in him. Leaders who lead from their deepest core values aren't willing to be dissuaded by the comments of others or the situations and circumstances around them. They are willing to both be inspired and be an inspiration to others who will do great things.

I believe you can have it all, but you just can't have it all today. I believe if you can see it, you can achieve it. True life balance for the complicated new era that we are walking into is only possible when you center yourself on the ideals found in your core. This translates into leading from your heart and not your head. When you lead in this way and trust, not only is financial security yours by faith, but your life is enriched by deeper, loving relationships, as well as projects and plans that come to fruition. There is so much power in choosing to become an affluent mind. Read this book again and mark it up. It's yours for the absorbing and to facilitate your transformational choices to be better in order to lead better.

Maybe you noticed a little golden thread weaving through this precious little book. It's the word *core*. Let's go back to that for a second. For years, I've been a businesswoman, executive, and high-level corporate consultant and coach. What I've witnessed over the last 23 years is that the most successful people, those who lead from their core power, have deliberately created a self-awareness that comes from years of mastering change or reframing negative thinking. This is what Jennifer and Kenny have in common. People like them create disciplines that amplify their core values and allow the best to be transmitted to the world. I'll teach you more about that in the next part of the book.

PART 2

From Mindset to Skillset

CHAPTER 4

Lessons from Coaching for Leadership & Success

Without self-discipline, success is impossible, period.
—Lou Holtz

Core-centric leadership is the essence of being led by a greater vision or calling, but it requires more than your affluent mindset. It also takes skill and passionate pursuit. Core-centered leaders know they can't go it alone. There are leaders meant to lead leaders, healers who are here to heal the healers, and coaches for the coaches. It takes consultants, coaches, confidantes, and community to extract and hone vision and make the unseen seen. We all need a village. There is no such thing as "self-made." In the over 10,000 hours of coaching and consulting I have under my belt, one thing has become very clear: the process of asking good questions of great leaders works.

In addition, effective, sustaining leadership requires organization and the disciplines—or skill sets with boundaries—to keep that state of order from unravelling. One of the key habits I've observed and have integrated in my own life is a daily morning leadership routine that involves reflection, prayer, or meditation before jumping into the day. It's the concept of filling the tank so I can drive the car all day. The rest of the disciplines noted here are secondary results of that power-up, connect-in morning ritual.

Generally, the executive peak performance coaching field takes a holistic approach by integrating life factors such as relationships, career, health, finances, and purpose into a client's overall life. The aspects of a person's life are inherently interwoven, so for most individuals, there must be a process of creating a balance or harmony among all of these facets while achieving success with specific goals.

Coaching is about deliberate focused change, and change is a process. Many times, I've been hired by a large company to focus on creating a framework or foundation for their business, and I end up working with an individual leader on certain aspects that are blocking growth inside the organization. Because the human mind is not segmented into life areas, our thinking, values, integrity, and past experience bleed into all areas of our life, including our job or vocation. Leadership mindset shifts naturally emerge to help restore passion, master communication and messaging, or relatability.

Leaders who need a breakthrough often need an outside question to help them flip the script of negative thoughts or deep-rooted beliefs. The leadership role is fraught with expectations, performance measures, and responsibilities.

True foundational leaders are continuously seeking ways to improve themselves, their business, and to engage those who are following them. Those deliberate changes generally result in ten professional disciplines that complement the affluent core-focused mindset. In this next section, you will answer self-coaching questions that can help you achieve an immediate breakthrough or begin to see areas of your life in which you can upgrade the skillset that supports your affluent mindset.

CHAPTER 5
The 10 Keys to Any Endeavor

Character cannot be developed in ease and quiet. Only through experiences of trial and suffering can the soul be strengthened, vision cleared, ambition inspired, and success achieved.
—Hellen Keller

Each of the following disciplines has invaluable influences on professional and personal success. They are addressed primarily to leaders because leadership starts with self. We must be leaders of ourselves before we can exceptionally lead others.

Then, there is the influence of others. This is about transforming an organization or group for the better. Ineffective, power-hungry managers often invert this principle and assume that the leader must be served by the people. Effective leadership is always about service, based on action and validated by results.

Integrate these ten keys, starting this week in your own life, and watch your life change for the better.

#1 VISION CASTING

If your actions inspire others to dream more, learn more,
do more and become more, you are a leader.
—John Quincy Adams

Vision Casting is an important professional discipline that springboards success in any profession. Vision is clearly seeing a future image of what you or your endeavor intend to become.

Leslie was a regional business development director for a major pharmaceutical company with a set of clear goals to "become the most profitable division in the company through personal excellence in customer service and sales. I was brought in to help her paint the picture of where she saw her company in three to five years. Casting her vision required the creation of a well-written communications plan, carefully defined for the purpose of working together and making it a reality. Once her team was on board behind her and helped to create the new customer service measures and tactics, upper management could be convinced of her leadership and let her move forward with budgeting for the new plan.

The vision keeps the train running because it's bigger than you. It's a measure point for performance, and it helps you pull the right players in the game as you keep them motivated and structured.

Vision Casting allows a person to see where they are going, to bridge the gap from where they are and where they want to be, and to help others join and follow them. In the case of a volunteer who quits or an employee who has to take a sudden leave of absence, the well-defined roles and details make it easier to send in a new player.

Vision Casting is a three-fold process:

1. *It requires a better future state.* Visions should be detailed in concept and contain sensory clarity, meaning you can almost touch, hear, smell, or taste it.

2. *It requires sharing.* You will want to communicate in such a way that you not only relate an "idea" of what the long-term plan looks like and who it will serve, but you help enroll them as a critical member of its execution.

3. *It requires repeating.* Everyone who is directly involved should *know* the vision of their department or company. Not read-about-it knowledge, but clarity of the vision itself. This is not simply a mission statement written down and forgotten, but real communication that's repeated using multiple methods. This applies especially for you, the vision caster. If you've done the work of detailing your vision and goals, ask yourself, "When was the last time I looked at them? Where is that old business plan?" Print out vision points and display them on your desk facing you. Pin them to the visor in your car to read whenever you're waiting. Stick them on the mirror in your bathroom at home to remind yourself daily of what to focus on. In any given day there is a lot of opportunity to do good, but only a slim chance of finishing what is great.

Coach Yourself Visionary:

- Is your vision detailed, actionable, and progressive?
- Is your vision true to your core values?

#2 DETERMINATION

If plan A doesn't work, the alphabet has 25
more letters—204 if you're in Japan.
—Claire Cook, Seven Year Switch

Determination is what gets you up earlier in the morning and keeps you focused when distractions fill your periphery. Determination is for those long-haul visions and dreams, where the enormity of time and tasks can overwhelm us. It's important when faced with the decision to keep going as the tedium threatens to slow us, distract us, and cause us to want to give up. The discipline of determination is necessary and needs practice. For executives, entrepreneurs, and leaders of non-profits with volunteers, determination is critical.

Don't necessarily mistake the difficulty of the task as some kind of sign it's not meant to be. Everything worth doing is going to have setbacks, and determination separates the courageous from the quitter. Who graduates from college without determination? Who starts a company and brings it to a sustaining growth or profit without the discipline of determination? Through visualization and reframing techniques, you can build the discipline of determination.

Coach Yourself Determined:

- A reframe is a way of seeing something in a new frame or a new light. It allows you to ask yourself a better question that helps you move from a negative situation to a positive one. It's a changing of the mind.
- How can I see (name the situation) in a better light?
- What am I learning from it?
- What must I now do to move forward?

#3 PERSEVERANCE

I have discovered in life that there are
ways of getting almost anywhere
you want to go, if you really want to go.
—Langston Hughes

Perseverance is often thought to be a quality or character trait. However, make no mistake, it is a learned and integrated *discipline*. It's something you choose in the face of hardship. You decide to go on, head down and teeth bared, to wait out the storm. The biggest difference between perseverance and persistence is that perseverance usually comes *from* hardship or *in spite* of hardship. It's steady, unyielding steadfastness in a course of action or purpose, especially when enveloped in difficulties, obstacles, or discouragement. It's what gets you moving in spite of pain and helps you face your staff or investors after a falter; it speaks to devotion and integrity. It's important to your success as a leader and in life because two things are certain: we will encounter trials, and we will receive blessings when we remain steadfast under trial.

Perseverance helps us see the rainbow after the storm and sometimes even during the storm. Perseverance requires a fixed, unwavering eye on the vision. Your vision casting efforts will be of great benefit at this time because those who share your vision can come alongside you to keep you facing forward. When you determine to persevere, you can refocus on the dream, vision, and purpose, knowing that you were endowed with the personality, skills, and experiences to make the vision come to pass. People will come with you due to your strength and endurance.

Coach Yourself Perseverant:

- A coach will refresh your mind of the vision, help you see the good in the difficult, help you reframe your circumstances so that you can change your perspective, and release your creativity to access alternative approaches, attitudes, and ideas that you can use as you persevere.
- Imagine a leader you admire right now. Imagine that you can talk to them about what they would do regarding a crisis you went through or are going through.
- Ask yourself how they would handle it.
- Congratulations! By accessing what you think your mentor would say, you have accessed your own answers.

#4 PERSISTENCE

If I had to select one quality, one personal characteristic that I regard as being most highly correlated with success, whatever the field, I would pick the trait of persistence. Determination. The will to endure to the end, to get knocked down seventy times and get up off the floor saying, "Here comes number seventy-one!"
—Richard M. DeVos

Persistence is often correlated with achievement. It's a requirement of any success or accomplishment. It's the principle illustrated in the story of the slow and steady turtle who wins the race. When you're persistent and you carry on the discipline of persistence in your life, you're able to take on bite-sized chunks day in and day out until you reach that end goal. Those big dreams of yours are worthy of trying and failing again until you get it right.

3 Insights about Persistence:

1. Persistence is a discipline because if we don't develop it by using it regularly, we won't have it when we need it most. It doesn't show up right when we need it unless it's already a discipline we're cultivating.

2. Persistence is associated with patience, which is another "p" word that falls somewhere between perseverance and pain on my "resistance scale." Yet, when we see how closely linked these two are, it gives us a clue into developing this discipline. Keeping at it sometimes means delaying gratification. Patiently working, and reworking when necessary, and not idle waiting is persistence.

3. Persistence is not the practice of insanity. You've heard the colloquial definition of insanity, which states: *insanity is doing the same thing the same way over and over and expecting different results.* Thomas Edison is often held as an example of true persistence. In American oral tradition, he apparently failed to create the incandescent light bulb more than 10,000 times before having success through persistence. What most of these references leave out is key: that Edison said himself when he reached experiment 9,999 that he was asked by a reporter, "Sir, are you going to fail 10,000 times?" Edison confidently replied, "I have not failed at each attempt; rather, I've succeeded at discovering another way not to invent an electric lamp." The point is that he adapted. He learned from each attempt and adapted. I love the line from Mike Norton in *Fighting for Redemption,* "Fall. Stand. Learn. Adapt." That illustrates what it is to persevere.

In a recent study, published by the *Journal of Finance* entitled: "Which CEO Characteristics and Abilities Matter?," the authors★ obtained detailed assessments of more than 300 CEO candidates. Through the detailed assessments, specific performance measurements, and interviews, each applicant was rated on more than 30 specific characteristics and abilities. What did they find? The most successful CEOs were those who were persistent, efficient, and proactive. Persistent leaders don't give up. They stick with assignments until they are done. Efficient CEOs get a lot done in a short period of time. And proactive ones are self-directed and regularly bring in new ideas.

If your "stick-to-it" button of persistence is not your strength, surround yourself with others who care. If patience is not your virtue, review the affluent mind acrostic to cultivate the frame of mind that frees you to tap back into your core. It's important to develop these skillsets day-by-day, little-by-little to create habits for life.

Coach Your Persistence:

- Ask yourself, "Do I have what it takes?"
- Who can be my rear guard and accountability partner to help me make it happen?

#5 HOPE

I dwell in possibility.
—Emily Dickinson

In a speaking engagement on leadership in 2010, I said that I define the word *hope* as an acronym meaning "heaps of pure expectation!" If you look up the word in any dictionary, you will see that hope is actually a synonym for expectation. Yet, in our modern-day culture, the definition almost seems like last resort thinking for bad times. The word carries with it an implicit expectation of something better to come, however, *of possibility.*

If, as a leader, you're accustomed to sidelining hope in favor of the more concrete to-do list and timeline, you're doing yourself a great disservice. Without hope in your vision and expectation in your goals, you really can't see the possibilities in what isn't yet a reality.

I've heard it said that hope is poor planning. This type of thinking is extremely limiting because it puts restrictions on the creative possibilities of process. Hope is what gives us the inspiration for something better, turns process into a journey, and turns a failure into impetus to try again. Leaders with hope inspire confidence, and forward-facing confidence emboldens creativity. Light the lamp in others by being a hope-filled leader.

We each have within us the capacity to generate hope. It's something we choose. Especially when it appears that there is no hope, it's critical that we stay mindful and intentional about nurturing hope in our own lives, as well as the lives of staff, volunteers, coworkers, family, and kids. As we deliberately associate ourselves into a feeling of hope, the expectation follows. And a hopeful attitude for any leader or influencer is contagious.

Coach Yourself Hopeful:

Think of a scenario in which you lost hope. You most likely did so because you believed some kind of lie. It's okay to be honest about something you feel holds you back personally. Maybe it's weight loss or addiction. Maybe it's a timely scenario, like hoping you receive a loan so that you can pay employees in your small business.

Now, remember a time when you came through a similar situation successfully. Write it down, and answer the following questions:

- What positive expectation can I have for this situation?
- Who do I need around me to stay anchored to hope?
- What quote or scripture can I memorize to anchor my mind with this positive outcome I envision?
- Each morning before prayer or meditation, visualize the best-case scenario and give thanks for it as if it's already done.

#6 ORGANIZATION

*The question of what you want to own is actually
the question of how you want to live your life.*
—Marie Kondo

Growing an organization starts with you being organized. Whether it's a non-profit, a corporation, or your own small business, there has to be a sense of organization and structure. This also applies to the free-thinking Bohemian artist who goes with the flow. If you're leading anyone, including yourself, a lack of organization will bury you.

Being organized is what I call a double positive. You get the benefits that being organized brings, such as more time to do the things you need to do. It gives you an ability to take an overview of process, flow, and what's working or needs tweaking. You gain a sense of balance and peace of mind. And just as important, you gain what you would have lost to disorganization—namely, missed appointments, lost paperwork, limited opportunities, difficulty in handling responsibilities, guilt, self-disdain, or imposter syndrome. You know that deep down, clutter blocks progress, and overwhelm stifles the creativity you need to lead.

Organization as a discipline means we're taking the time daily to do things that matter. If this is a weakness for you, recognize it, forgive it and address it. How you address it might include hiring a person to keep you organized, such as an administrative assistant, coach, or professional organizer. If you're ready to be more organized, there are many books, podcasts, and organizations that can help you create a structure of where things go, a disciplined approach to getting them in their places, and a time management system that works for you.

Coach yourself Organized:

- There are many facets of organization, such as keeping an up-to-date calendar, filing, keeping a clean work area, and many others that may apply to what you do.
- Which organization tactics do you need to incorporate today?
- If your to-do list is too long, what can be delegated or deleted to increase your productivity?

#7 COMMUNICATION

Words of course are the most powerful drug used by mankind.
—Rudyard Kipling

Effective communication is the art of getting your ideas across in a way that can be understood by the receiver. Through effective communication, we better understand a person or situation, are able to resolve differences, build trust and respect, and develop environments where creative ideas, problem-solving, affection, and caring can thrive.

Communication is 100% the responsibility of the communicator. It's not 50-50. You might be thinking, "What about the receiver's responsibility for understanding?" As a communicator, you have no control over them and certainly not of their understanding. Your control rests with your ability to be as effective as possible.

As a leader, communication is the primary way to enroll, persuade, direct, inform, educate, mentor, and develop rapport with others. The issue is that others don't share your personality. If they need to be taught the vision and how they fit in, they need your understanding of their strengths and weaknesses. So, it's critical to communicate in a listener-focused manner. Making sure you're effective is worth the extra time.

In the information age, there are so many ways to communicate and even more opportunities for misunderstandings. Although we live in an age where we send, receive, and process huge numbers of messages every day, effective communication is more than exchanging information. Effective communication combines a set of skills including nonverbal communication, attentive listening, and the ability to recognize and understand your own emotions/talents and personality, as well as those of the person you're communicating with. Begin with practicing with your immediate inner circle, such as your own family or friends.

Effective Communication Requires:

1. Active Engaged Listening

Beyond just understanding the words and information, listening also means tuning in to the speaker's emotions about what they are communicating. Engaged listening focuses on the speaker, their body language, context, nonverbal clues, tone, and what they *don't* say. Active listening avoids interrupting and allows the speaker to not just finish their sentence, but complete their thought. Withhold the appearance of any judgment, blame, or opinion while they are speaking. This helps you, the listener, better focus on what they're telling you because you're not lost in your own snap judgments. And when you set aside your judgment to fully understand a person, even the most difficult communication can lead to a profound connection.

2. Nonverbal Communication

Pay attention to the wordless clues such as body movements, facial expressions, gestures, eye contact or lack of eye contact, posture, the tone in the voice, and even muscle tension and breathing. The way a person looks, listens, moves, and reacts to another person communicates more about how they're feeling than their words alone.

This goes for both the receiver's body language and the communicator's body language.

I'm not talking about the touchy-feely stuff parodied in the movies. This is self-awareness and self-actualization for the purpose of managing your own feelings, actions, and reactions in a communication setting. That is, taking responsibility for your own emotions and understanding. You can achieve positive and tangible results if you improve your self-awareness during communication.

3. Written communication

Written exchanges such as texting, emails, and various forms of social media can trip up communication and create misunderstandings and resentments. An effective communicator who employs active listening and self-awareness disciplines will adapt these skills to written communications.

Coach Yourself Communicative:

- Who are the people closest to me who seem to misunderstand me the most?
- What can I do to begin to make myself understood?

#8 TIME MASTERY

Time = Life, therefore, waste your time and waste your life,
or master your time and master your life.
—Alan Lakein

This professional discipline to springboard success may seem a bit obvious. After all, managing our time as a resource responsibility goes with the territory of leadership. It means choosing to steward important moments in every area of your life. By mastering time, not just managing it, you are in essence developing a discipline of spending every amount of energy with intention. Intentional living requires knowing yourself, knowing what you want in your life, and some understanding of your purpose, followed by choices that reflect those priorities. It means not allowing time to escape or control you. It doesn't mean life without fun or spontaneity. Instead, it ensures that you can really enjoy yourself without a cloud composed of "should" and "ought-to" thoughts sitting on your shoulder.

But don't make an idol of your to-do list because then, it will never end. Think of it simply as a "capture list." Now, take that capture list and schedule the key items according to priority to get them completed or delegated within a certain timeframe. When you begin mastering your time, you can still use a time management system that works for you. But then, you'll understand that your time also includes time-wasters such as moments spent worrying, sleeplessness, procrastination, distractions, and interruptions. Choosing a mastery approach intentionally replaces most of these wasters with useful alternatives.

Time in line, for example, is an opportunity to catch up on some reading. Interruptions become opportunities.

Notice the method and type of interruption and make changes to curtail it next time. Make the shift to thinking about the positives, the blessings, and the things to be thankful for in place of worries. Allow creativity to flow for a way forward through any mess, which may be exactly what you need to combat the things that worry you. This is why time mastery is a discipline because it requires conscious and intentional choices for both our actions and our thinking.

Coach Yourself to Time Mastery:

- Do you constantly find yourself needing more time?
- If you answered yes, list the 3 big things you want to do by the end of the year. Then, schedule them in your calendar weekly as something to work on. Maybe it's dropping 20 pounds, so you schedule 3 visits a week to a gym. Or perhaps it's writing a book, so you pick an hour a day to write.

#9 DELEGATION

*If you delegate tasks, you create followers. If you
delegate authority, you create leaders.*
—Craig Groeschel

Good delegation is a leadership discipline and a must if
you're going to be effective. It's a brilliant discipline that
simultaneously saves you time, develops and grooms your
people, and motivates them. Lack of delegation or poor
delegation will frustrate you, demotivate your staff, and
cause you to fail to achieve the task or purpose.

Delegation works well with vision casting and requires
good communication. It tells someone that you trust them
to complete a task in a way that serves the purpose, and it
allows you to truly multitask and accomplish more.

Often, leaders try to keep things in a place of perfection
that they have created. It stifles their ability to free up time for
attending to the most important matters. It stifles the creativity
of the recipient of the delegated task. Delegation should
stimulate a new and creative process, freeing up one person to
focus their energy elsewhere and entrusting another to bring
the shared task along. Your vision is not only being cast through
the minds of the parties, it's being cast through the hands, feet,
and voices of others and is a propagator for efficiency.

A leader's approach to delegation in their own life
includes their attitude and ability to let go.

Coach Yourself to Delegate:

- What can you hand over now?
- What do you need to loosen your grip on to free
  up your own time?

#10 COACHING

Life can only be understood backwards;
but it must be lived forwards.
—Soren Kierkegaard

Being coachable (different from teachable) is a discipline for success in the life of every leader. The value of cultivating this discipline is priceless, for its payoff will positively impact your leadership, personal success, relationships, and family. To truly be coachable, leaders need to drop the mask of infallibility and over-the-top confidence to instead embrace *humility.* Passion is great. Zeal is great. Persistence is great. Plans are great. But without changing mindsets that hold you back, you can't move past certain mental barriers or break free from ingrained self-sabotage.

Sometimes, you need others to ask the right question. Other times, you can read a book like this and act on the exercises. The result? You come up with your best answers and break free of negative feedback loops that hold you back from moving forward with a smooth path set before you.

"Coachability" involves your ability to *trust.* Can you give up control and try something new, even if you don't think it will work? For leaders used to being in control, this can take some time to cultivate. Trust might also include an ability to *suspend what you think you know* in order to embrace what you're learning. In this way, leaders who have been frustrated, overworked, overwhelmed, or "in the weeds" can begin to see the light again.

On the flip side, to be a good coach for those around you, take time to ask great questions and then listen for key attitudes and indicators of where each person is in their growth process. Look for where they have resistance, resilience, and readiness to move forward. Here's the critical next part: you listen not to give advice but to formulate anther great question. Coaching is a means to non-judgmentally help others grow in a manner that is uniquely and creatively their own. The process of coaching means you presuppose that the person you are coaching has the answers on the inside. Non-leading questions bring that answer out, and people are set free.

Coaching provides a positive position from which the person being coached, such as an employee, a volunteer, or your daughter, will not feel judged or ridiculed. It's a space for them to learn. Because it's question-based and non-accusatorial, the person being coached can explore alternatives in how they approach things, consider different attitudes, examine their decisions, and progress creatively.

Coaching enhances emotional intelligence and brings you up to a higher level of values-based thinking in whatever area in your life you deem necessary. As you widen the breadth of you, it makes you a better leader—the kind others want to follow.

Coach yourself, Coach:

This week, when someone needs advice, remind yourself to *ask* a non-leading *question* that leaves them with their own best answers and helps them feel empowered.

PART 3

*Drawing from
a Deeper Well*

CHAPTER 6

Matter, Moxie, and Muse

We've talked about Mindset and Skillset. Now, let's talk about what I call "Valueset." The first two sections of this book were designed to inspire you to remember and tap into the core values that create an affluent mind, as well as develop the discipline to sustain and support that mindset. Eventually, we all trip up and fall prey to circumstances. We need to be reminded of who we truly are within our core.

Over the last eleven years, while studying the clinical effects of burnout, the psychology of happiness, and the transformative principles behind leadership and coaching, I've observed a thread of body-mind-spirit connectedness between science and faith as they apply to business. Regardless of whether we consider ourselves religious or spiritual, or not, the human psyche always relentlessly pursues a connection with a higher principle. Almost all great leaders align these three elements: (1) their lives and work, which have to do with the physical body—Matter and Skillset; (2) the Moxie that drives them from within, which is their determined mission and Mindset; and (3) the Muse that lights them up, which is the inspiration of the small guiding voice of Spirit or their *Valueset*.

There is a body, mind, spirit connection in all of us, and when these three tangible and intangible parts of ourselves align, we become an empowered, unstoppable force. But that requires keeping these aspects in balance as much as possible. When these parts of us aren't aligned and balanced, we feel out of sorts and begin to seek help because we know something isn't right.

Balancing our lives is an elusive concept, however. Almost every work-life balance program implemented in big corporations boils down to taking a day off when needed, using up our vacation days every year because they won't roll over, or calling the mental health helpline to engage an insurance-provided therapist. It only occurs to us to consider balance when life is moving too fast for too long, and we finally feel the pressures of life *physically*. Here are some early warning signs of physical and mental burnout:

Mental—maybe you begin to make statements like this to others:

- I'm so exhausted.
- I need a day off.
- I should create some kind of mediation practice.
- I wake up tired.
- I need a vacation, but I have too many deadlines right now.
- I can't seem to get my message across to others.
- I can't handle what's going on in the news, so I tune it out.
- I don't have the energy or time to exercise.

Physical—you may experience stress leading to:

- Chest pain or cardiovascular disorders such as dysrhythmia
- GI upset (chronic diarrhea or constipation)
- Weight gain
- Using alcohol, drugs, or food as a means of escape
- Experiencing anxiety or even panic attack

As these warning signs begin to surface, we tend to brush them off and keep going with our busy schedules. Yet, burnout is one of the global pandemics we have ignored for far too long.

There are glimpses of balance in all of our lives— moments when we notice *flow*. Suddenly, our time is managed, and our confidence rises briefly. Then, life occurs again. An unforeseen event like a traffic jam, a missed airplane flight, or a last-minute impossible deadline throws us off course once again.

How can we reframe the situation so that we stay grounded, in peace, and true to our core when life goes haywire and throws us off center?

Reinventing the Wheel

From the time I became an entrepreneur, I started walking the path of personal development. In an intense period of three years between 2004 and 2007, I devoured multiple leadership, development, and coaching certification courses. One of my favorite personal development exercises was mapping out and ranking my own life balance wheel at one of the many events I attended. It was like looking at a long forgotten, full-length mirror, showing me an immediate and even scary glimpse of my gaps and weaknesses versus my strengths. But something wasn't fully developed about it.

Maybe you've also worked with one of these life-balance wheels. You form the inside of a pie chart representing your life areas and rank each area of your life on a scale from 1-10. You rank some areas better than others and end up with a pinwheel that seems to prove how out of balance you are.

There are two solutions presented in coaching the outcome of this wheel. One says if we continue to lead from our strengths, we'll pull up all the other areas of our wheel. But that doesn't work in practice. If I'm unhappy in my marriage, for example, how will increasing my finances make a difference? Improving my finances won't even help me if I dislike my occupation unless I use the money to help me *change* occupations.

The other typical solution instructs us to fill in the gaps as we discover our weaknesses. I don't know about you, but as a busy leader, I prefer to delegate tasks related to my weaknesses.

The truth is that these traditional balance wheels have never matched up with my life categories, nor have they accounted for how the various areas of my life affect each other, whether positively or negatively.

Here's what I mean: imagine for a moment that each section of your wheel is filled in with a color. Place the wheel on a carnival spinner until the colors begin to move into other areas. When the spinner stops, you see a blurred mosaic of color streaks that have bled through the lines. This is how life actually looks. We might isolate aspects of our life, but in reality, they affect each other. But as I said, that doesn't mean simply lifting one area will automatically lift another. It's more complicated than that.

The other thing that bothered me about the traditional wheel was that the spiritual piece of the pie was just another wedge. This is the part of my life that encompasses my artistic, creative spirit—my essential connection to God, Divine Intelligence, Spirit, (or whatever term you use). As I began to pray about this, I realized that my spirituality actually encompasses all areas of my life—or it certainly should. It's the *core* of who I am, not just one wedge among all the others. And I wanted that core to permeate all aspects of my life. I wanted that kind of integral authenticity—my Valueset—everywhere I walked, whether in my career or in my personal relationships.

After remaining frustrated with these wheels for a while, I *received* the solution in 2009. It came in the form of what I can only describe as a massive, instant divine download. I drew it on my whiteboard, looked up in awe and said, "Thank You, God." It answered all of my questions at once, and it continues to grow, adapt, and evolve as the solution to our modern work-life balance dilemma.

I began to use it with clients and teach it in my leadership programs and masterminds, all with great results. This framework is a tool you can use in an instant to reboot how you observe and respond to the problems you face.

The Core Wheel I created isn't about fine-tuning our lives for a constant state of balance. It's about taking a snapshot of our life in its current complexities and using it to make adjustments. We'll find that we need to let go of some areas, things, habits, or people, while we need to hang onto others. Some of the adjustments we make may be small, but they can often provide big results. Other shifts are massive and required to play our long game and achieve lasting change.

I teach my clients to come back to this balance wheel again and again as a means of self-checking their priorities and values as they align or misalign with their goals and purpose. It's the first of several wheels I've developed that we refer to as "The Core Wheelhouse."

The initial Core Wheel has three concentric circles or areas, along with eight segments. It illustrates the complexity of life from a body–mind–spirit/holistic/intangible perspective. At the same time, it compartmentalizes the tangible and ongoing major areas of our lives. Finally, you have an image for what your glorious, multifaceted, complex life looks like! And this image helps you see and dissect it all at once in a simple diagram.

My first drawing of the wheel looked like this with God in the center, but as years progressed and I used it inside fortune 500 companies and non-profits to help transform deflated leadership teams, I kept referring to the word core. I would ask what's in your *core*? What are your core values? Where do they come from? How can you align your projects and tactics accordingly? How can we create KPIs and metrics to ensure that employees are engaged with your corporate core values as well as their own? Let's define it. For both your company and you personally. I taught it to thousands of individuals in over 12 countries in my programs. We rebranded as Corepreneur in 2018 and it stuck so that anyone could use it regardless of personal belief systems.

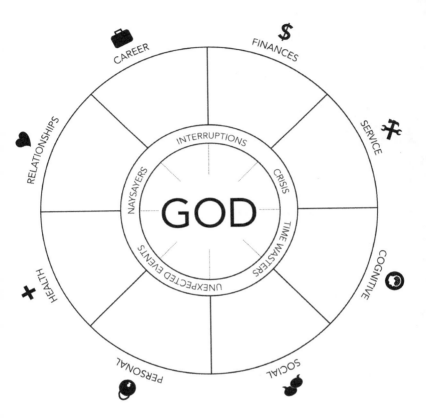

Figure 1 – My Original Life-In-Balance Wheel

On the modified wheel with C-O-R-E in the center, standing for Centered, Open, Resilient, and Energized, look at the layers from the outside in as Body (Matter), Mind (Moxie), and Spirit (Muse) illustrated like this:

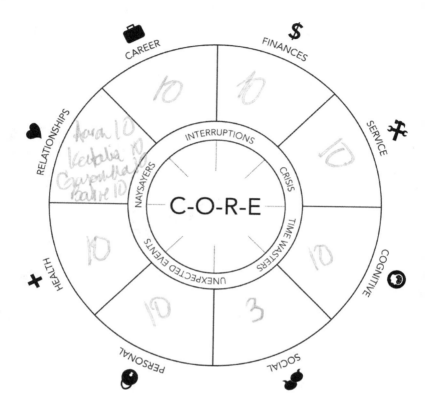

Figure 2: The C-O-R-E Wheel

Starting from the outside boundary, there are eight divisions representing each of the areas of life. These are the compartments we can see, feel, touch, and measure. They are what make up a life, but they don't represent what drives us. That's reserved for the core.

Moving inward, the next concentric area is a kind of enemy territory or minefield that I call "the gray matter." It deals with the deepest recesses of our mind. It runs through each area of our life and includes our thoughts and reactions to the joy-stealers and time-wasters that draw us away from our highest and best expression. This is the disruptive place within us that's most vulnerable to a negative pull from naysayers, crises, interruptions, and unexpected events.

The biggest battles we come up against are the ones we fight in our minds, and they take place right here in this gray area. This is the area of our mind, will, emotions, ego, and choices. It's where the thoughts we think become the words we speak and the actions we take in the outer section. If we don't reframe our thoughts, we're bombarded with negative ones that create strife and chaos. This section illustrates how a person can look like they have it all but still be a tormented soul.

Besides gray matter, I call this section "Moxie" because that's what it can be in its most positive form. We have an opportunity in the gray matter to choose to be fearless and loving rather than the opposite. In short, when our mind is controlled by our Valueset in our core, we have peace.

The core in the center is the part of our lives that's anchored by divine protection, fresh inspiration, and spiritual vision. It's where our lives are inherently centered, open, resilient, and energized. It crosses every area of our life in a positive way, whether we recognize it or not. It's where our spirit mingles with the Spirit of God and finds comfort, wisdom, understanding, and a host of other goodies.

When we stand in the gray area and look outward, we feel frazzled. When we stand there and go deeper into our core, we feel safe. Once refreshed by our Muse, we can re-enter the gray area and pick our Moxie back up.

Coaching Yourself Through the Wheel

From the center point outward, each area of your life will be ranked on a scale of 1-10. You have a major home-field advantage, however, compared to the commonly used life balance wheel variations that leave you high and dry, thirsting for balance. The center—your core, your Valueset—is always there. Like the South Pole, it's a magnetic positive pole.

Beginning at the center of the wheel, define the following: What's in your C-O-R-E? In other words, what do you do to tap into your core power and activate your Valueset when your circumstances go crazy and your gray matter chimes in, diminishing your Moxie? This is your positive pole that keeps you grounded, centered, and focused. It's your inner sanctuary and filling station, and your newfound awareness of it is the game-changer.

Define it for yourself by answering these questions:

1. What are your top five core values? (Love, Peace, Joy, etc.)

   Freedom

   Accomplishment

   Family

   Affluence

   Peace

2. Who or what do you name your inspiration or Muse? (God, Higher Power, Spirit, Universal Intelligence, etc.) Name it based on what feels right in your core right now.

The Universe

3. How do you tap into your Muse? Do you read a good book and let your mind be taken away with inspired, fearless characters? Do you walk in nature, pray, meditate, read the Bible or other spiritual text, listen to an inspiring podcast or sermon, listen to soft music, or practice gratitude journaling or laughter therapy?

Meditation
Read Inspirational
Books

4. Now, let's explore more about your gray matter. Write
    down your top five time-wasters and joy-stealers. Perhaps
    you have some acute naysayers, crises, interruptions, or
    unexpected events that are affecting you right now.
    What is robbing you of your Moxie and making it more
    difficult for you to stay centered in your core?

Doubter

Naysayer

Negative Voice

Debbie Downer

Worry Wart

5. Next, let's explore what's in your core. Begin to rank each
    life area from the inside out on a scale of 1-10. For example,
    starting with the cognitive section, start on the line right
    above the word "time-wasters," and rank that area based
    on your habits or reality most of the time. The answers are
    neutral, so be honest in your ranking. Before you do so,
    however, read the brief description of each below, starting
    with "cognitive" and going around clockwise, to help you
    give yourself a more accurate rating.

_____

_____

_____

_____

Cognitive: How are you feeding and challenging your mind? Are the books you're reading, the music you're listening to, and the words you're hearing and saying feeding your soul or causing you stress?

Social: This section refers to your secondary relationships— your friends, extended family, and coworkers. This is where that family member you haven't spoken to in a couple of years will fit in. How do you feel about your extended social life? Do you spend enough time with friends, or are you too busy for them? Does your social life consist mainly of work or work friends? How do you spend your time when you're with friends and family? How often do you see them? Are you on Facebook or other social media? Are your interactions with others restricted to your time on social media? Do you feel you can be authentic in these secondary relationships, or do you feel you have to hide parts of yourself?

Personal: I call this the "my house in order" segment. It's about our personal care and feeding. Do you find it difficult to define the aspects of your personal life because it has all but given way to your career and caring for others like your spouse and children? Do you feel it's selfish to care for yourself? I had a client who felt that way, but once she was able to see the necessity of self-care, it changed the entire tone of her home and led to improved relationships with her husband and children. To evaluate this area, ask yourself: Is your physical house in order? What does your desk look like? What kind of self-care do you do for yourself regularly? Do you take daily walks? What makes you smile? What do you look forward to doing, and when was the last time you did it? What are your indulgences?

Health: What are you doing for your health? Do you exercise regularly? What does your diet look like; are you eating well? Are you struggling with your weight? Have you had an annual physical? If so, how were your lab results? Do you have any ongoing health problems, and are you attending to them or ignoring them? Do you consider your body to be a temple?

Relationships: Are you satisfied with your closest core relationships? These would be your partner and children, or the few people who know you best. Ideally, these are the people you truly trust. Are these relationships contentious or harmonious? I suggest writing down each person you would place in this category and ranking your satisfaction with each relationship from 1-10 to determine an average for this section.

Career: Do you have a job or a career? Is it a vocation and/or your dream career? Do you enjoy it, or is it a drudge? If money were no object, if time were no object, and your education were of no consequence, would you be doing what you're currently doing . . . or something else? What do you see as your mission, vision, and purpose in life? Is your current job aligned with that mission, vision, and purpose? If you aren't sure, don't worry. This is something to continue to contemplate. If you do know, what would you be doing if you were fulfilling your purpose?

Finances: Are you satisfied with your financial state? Do you feel abundant or deprived? How far are you from the financial state you wish to have? Do you have an accountant, or do you take care of your own finances? Do you keep your checkbook balanced? Do you have a bank you can rely on? Do you pay your bills on time, or do you struggle to pay them? Are you in debt or living within your means? What are your financial goals in terms of your savings, 401K, investments, life insurance, and more? Are you on course to reach those goals?

Service: Do you give back to the community? Do you feel that your career serves others? Are you in a state of heart fulfillment and overflow so that you can serve or volunteer in a way that's congruent with your core? What would it take to get you to that state? If you aren't currently giving back, what organizations or charities would you enjoy serving?

6. When you have ranked all of the outer aspects of your wheel, take a look. How balanced is it? If your wheel were on a car, would it be a bumpy ride? For most of us, it is pretty bumpy until we begin to consciously and consistently work on balance. So ask yourself: What weak areas are negatively impacting the other areas of your life? Conversely, what strong areas are positively impacting the other areas of your life?

Pretty good

Some work a Socid

———————————————————

———————————————————

———————————————————

Here are a couple of examples. Linda, one of the members of our Corepreneur Academy, was a runner who ate a very healthy diet. Her physical health was one of her key strengths, which helped her career thrive. This, in turn, influenced her finances. Her health allowed her to work longer hours and maintain a keen focus, which led to two promotions. Her health also gave her the extra energy to start a side business that she'd always wanted to try.

Eighteen months later, however, Linda's side business had grown so much that she no longer made the time to exercise consistently or eat well. She was so busy that she started to grab fast food in order to keep the pace of her work. In addition, she rarely got more than six hours of sleep. As a result of her diminished health, the other areas of her wheel were weakening. In order to get back in balance, she scheduled workouts and refused the junk food that had become a habit.

Then, there's Jemma. Her marriage was in trouble, which caused her career and her relationship with her children to deteriorate. Suffering in limbo in an abusive situation wasn't working for her, so in order to move on, she felt she had to make the decision to file for a divorce. This would cause her finances to diminish for a while, but she knew she'd be able to bring that into balance in time.

7. As you review the areas that are weakening or strengthening others, write down two adjustments you want to make to begin to bring your life back into balance. As you succeed with those, you can move on to other adjustments to begin to get your wheel in shape so that your life is a smoother ride.

_____

_____

_____

_____

_____

_____

As you work through this process, you'll find that this tool, along with what you've learned throughout this book, will help you develop and sustain an Affluent Mind.

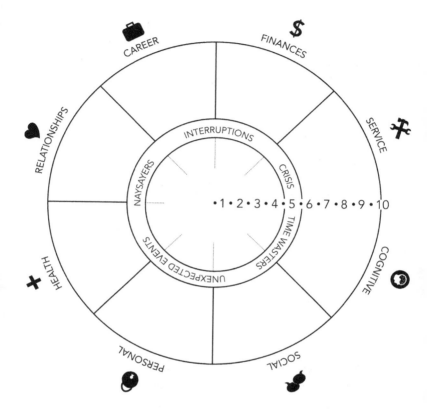

Figure 3: Score Your Core

Here's what you know now:

- Your core is infinitely full and knowledgeable
- You are complete from the inside out.
- The external is temporary.

- The internal is infinite and forever; a deep well to draw wisdom and strength from in every situation.
- The greatest leaders lead from within, and so can you starting right now.

You Can Continue This Process. . .

I'm currently writing a full-length book on this process, so watch for that. In the meantime, you can explore it further in our Corepreneur Academy Program and hear from core centered leaders in the Corepreneur Podcast. See the Resources section at the end of the book for more information.

CONCLUSION

The best and brightest leaders have affluent minds that are centered, open, resilient, and energized. When you lead from your core, your affluent mindset can serve in the midst of the darkest times. I have dedicated my life to training global leaders. At the publishing of this book in 2020, your light and leadership are needed now more than ever. The stock market is low, so it's seemingly a great time to buy. In the same vein, if you've lost your job, it isn't the time to be swept up in the external flood. It's time to self-nurture and shift your mindset so that you emerge successful.

If you resist getting swept up in the chaos and overwhelm of life during troubled times, smooth sailing will return, and you will become you—upright, and stronger than before. Although we will remember 2020 as the year of COVID and chaos, these timeless principles help us daily, regardless of the issues, time-wasters, energetic vampires, health issues, and the unexpected events that we all encounter. Don't you deserve a happy balanced life?

ABOUT THE AUTHOR

Anne Arvizu, PharmD, FASCP, PCC, is a business advisor and globally recognized expert in leadership, operations strategy, and organizational design. She is the founder and CEO of Corecentryx, Inc, a professional leadership and development consulting firm specializing in productivity, executive skill certification and advancement of gender parity. Her expertise, business advisory and *Corepreneur*® brands now span the Fortune 500 C-suites of multiple industries and the non-profit sector. Anne founded her first successful niche-market company, RxER Communications Corp, in 2004 as a medical communications firm partnering with biotech clients. With more than 22 years of executive leadership experience in Biopharma arena, she is the most sought-after independent expert pharmacist in her category of patient-centric medical information.

Dr. Arvizu has served in key senior executive and global leadership roles, such as global head of Medical Information for Baxter International and Baxalta Pharmaceuticals, regional head of Medical Communications for GlaxoSmithKline, and former Board Member and Officer for the Board of Directors of the American Medical Writers Association. As an advocate for community health and social responsibility, she also gives back as chairperson of the South Florida YMCA Board of Advisors in her community.

Anne is a sought-after keynote speaker, author, and awarded biotech veteran. Recent awards include the 2020 Healthcare Businesswomen's Association (HBA) Luminary Award and she has been nominated for the Top 100 Healthcare Leaders award for 2020 by the International Forum on Advancements in Healthcare (IFAH).

Her passion is at the helm of Corepreneur Academy, a global leadership community for core-centered entrepreneurial executive women. Her radio program, The *Corepreneur* Podcast, is a must listen for executive level thought leaders looking to escape the mental paradigms of corporate dissatisfaction and live a life of freedom, autonomy, impact, and legacy. Anne brings leadership conversations to the table, as well as first-hand war stories of burnout and ultimate turnaround.

Anne currently provides private advisory as well as team

train-the-trainer initiatives to individuals and select fortune 500 companies and health care related organizations, while residing between her homes in South Florida. The companies she builds and the affiliations she keeps all share a common focus of promoting productivity, health, and life balance in the lives of entrepreneurial executives.

ACKNOWLEDGEMENTS

Thank you to my editors, especially Melanie Votaw. Special thanks also to Morgan Judy, Jeff Stevens, Bob DeGroff, Jeff Slone, and the fantastic editorial, agreements, design and marketing teams at Archway Publishing, a division of Simon & Schuster. Amazing. You are *all* Affluent Minds.

Special thanks to Carole Delorme, Debbie Boumans and Belinda Beaumont, for encouraging me to write this book the night it was conceived at GNO. You are loved and appreciated.

Behind every great woman is a great woman, mine is Suzanne Crise. Sincere gratitude for your support and trust over the past several years.

Alexa, Jamie and Ian Arvizu, always stay true to your core and lead from your infinitely informed hearts. All my love.

RESOURCES

Free Resources

- Need an affluent-minded community?
    - For more information, visit <u>AnneArvizu.com</u> and sign up for Anne's masterclass, connect via social media
- Is the corporate life or mindset of overwhelm no longer for you?
    - Download your *free* corporate-to-freedom checklist
- Burnout is an insidious slow killer, and it could be ruining your health and eroding your bottom line. Are you suffering burnout?
    - Take the *free* susceptibility quiz at <u>AnneArvizu.com</u>
- Build your business, balance your life and leave your leadership legacy.
- Never miss an episode of the Corepreneur® Podcast. Real inspirational stories of overcoming the chaos and overwhelm and challenges of corporate life and entrepreneurship, featuring today's top luminaries and business mentors.

- Subscribe to Anne's podcast on Apple Podcasts, iTunes, Stitcher or any other major digital radio outlet.
  - https://annearvizu.com/applepodcasts

Other Resources

Corepreneur® Academy – Amplify Your Leadership and Elevate the Lives you Touch

Corepreneur® Academy is *"The Fast Track from Corporate to Freedom"* for entrepreneurial executive leaders making the mindset leap from "corp to preneur." Lead from your core to live and give more.

Using The C-O-R-E Method, and the multiple wheels we have created in our C-O-R-E Wheelhouse helps burned out executives follow their passion, learn key business and entrepreneurial skills fast, connect with their true purpose and passion, and lead from their C-O-R-E so that they can be free of negative corporate paradigms—like the staunch old concept of "hard work ethic," which included too much time at the office. The new world we are living in requires a new way to be, lead and innovate the solutions the world needs most now.

Executive Advisory – When you need a personal guide for your life and business.

Go to AnneArvizu.com, and book a Strategy Call to help overcome a pressing problem. You may also book a Strategy VIP Day with Anne to map out your business success blueprint.

From The C-O-R-E® Retreat – The New Way to Be and Lead.

> This once a year, invitation only, 3-day immersion event is a revamp for your leadership and reset for your life. Learn more at AnneArvizu.com

CPSIA information can be obtained
at www.ICGtesting.com
Printed in the USA
BVHW030047030920
587786BV00005B/230